Coming Home
to Yourself

HARMONY BOOKS
NEW YORK

Coming Home to Yourself

A Meditator's Guide to Blissful Living

OSHO

A Meditator's Guide to Blissful Living
Copyright © 2020
OSHO International Foundation www.osho.com/copyrights
Osho image copyright © OSHO International Foundation
All rights reserved.

Published in the United States by Harmony Books, an imprint of the
Crown Publishing Group, a division of Penguin Random House LLC, New York.
crownpublishing.com

Harmony Books is a registered trademark, and the Circle colophon is a
trademark of Penguin Random House LLC.

OSHO® is a registered trademarks of Osho International Foundation
www.osho.com/trademarks

The text excerpts in this book are selected from various talks by Osho, given to a live
audience. All of Osho's talks have been published in full as books, and are also available
as original audio recordings. Audio recordings and the complete text archive can be
found via the online OSHO Library at osho.com/library

Library of Congress Cataloging-in-Publication Data has been applied for.

Printed in China

Book and cover illustrations by: Cecilia Turchelli
Design: Benedetto Degli Innocenti
Cover design by Sonia Persad

ISBN 978-1-984-82681-7

10 9 8 7 6 5 4 3 2 1

First Edition

CONTENTS

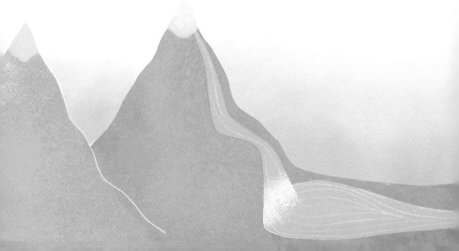

HOW TO USE THIS BOOK

*Move with as much wholeness and totality as you can
to the very center of your being, the center of the
cyclone. And you have come home.*
—Osho

All of us have experienced moments of "coming home"—feeling
relaxed, grounded, free of the restlessness that characterizes so
much of our everyday lives. These moments can arise in nature or in
the depths of an activity we enjoy, alone or together with people we
love. As unique and varied as the individuals who experience them,
these moments have in common the feeling that we are exactly
where we are supposed to be.

These pages, selected from Osho's hundreds of public talks and
intimate conversations, are designed to be a companion on the journey
toward transforming our rare moments of "at-home-ness" into an
undercurrent that permeates all aspects of our lives. They offer general
guidance about meditation and specific techniques to try, insights into
the habits that keep us tense and conflicted, and what life might look
like if we can recognize those habits and let them go.

In a very real sense, "how to use this book" is up to you. If you're
the sort of person who likes to read the manual before operating
the equipment, you can do that and read the book straight through
before experimenting with the techniques. If you're more the type to
jump straight into an activity to see what happens, you can do that,
too—although you may find yourself going back to read the parts you
skipped over to see how your experience fits in.

A brief practical note: You will find occasional references to
one or more of Osho's unique "active meditations" such as Dynamic,
Kundalini, or Nataraj. More information about these techniques can
be found at the back of the book.

A CERTAINTY

I know that if you jump into the stream you will be able to swim, because swimming is a natural phenomenon. One need not learn it. I'm not talking about the outer stream and swimming; there you may be drowned. I am talking about the stream of the inner consciousness, the stream of consciousness—if you jump into it. And that's what is meant, that is the parallel story that you have to decode. You naturally know. Have you ever seen any fish learning to swim?

Once Mulla Nasruddin was caught fishing somewhere that fishing was prohibited. The inspector came suddenly and he was caught red-handed: he was just hauling in a fish. He immediately threw the fish back and sat there, undisturbed. The inspector was standing there. He asked, "What are you doing, Mulla?" Mulla said, "I am teaching this fish to swim."

Now, no fish needs to be taught swimming. The fish is born there, swimming is like breathing. Who has taught you breathing?

There is no need to be afraid; if you are ready to trust, to jump into the stream of your consciousness, you will know how to swim. At the most, it can happen that you may drift a long way before a fisherman hauls you up. You can at the most drift, that's all. You cannot be drowned. You belong to consciousness, you are part of that stream.

AN INVITATION

Bliss is not pleasure; pleasure is physical, momentary. Bliss is not happiness, either; happiness is psychological—a little deeper than pleasure, but only a little. Pleasure is just on the surface and happiness is skin-deep, but just scratch the skin and it disappears. It has no real roots, it is just in the mind.

Bliss is neither of the body nor of the mind; hence it has infinite depth. It is your very soul, your self-nature, your being. Pleasure comes and goes; happiness happens and disappears. Bliss is forever. Even when we are not aware of it, it is there, present as an undercurrent; one just has to dig.

And that's my whole work here, to help to dig a well within your being so that you can find the undercurrent of blissfulness.

When you dig deep within yourself, first you will find truth, then you will find consciousness, and then you will find bliss. Bliss is the deepest—and the deepest is also the highest.

God is only a name for bliss. God is not a person. The very idea of God as a person has misled humanity. It is an experience, the experience that is beyond bodymind, the experience of that which is hidden in you and has always been there. You need not create it; you need not search for it anywhere else; you just have to dive deep within yourself.

To search means a turning in, it means exploring your interiority. I am not against the exterior—the exterior is beautiful—but if you don't know your interiority, if you don't know your inner world, your exterior cannot be very beautiful. It can have depth, beauty, joy, only if you are rooted within your own sources.

If a tree wants to reach high into the sky, wants to touch the stars and whisper with the clouds, then the first thing it has to do is to reach as deep into the earth with its roots, as deep as possible.

The deeper the roots, the higher the tree can rise. And the same is true about the internal and the external: the deeper the roots into the internal, the greater will be your approach into the external.

If your roots are really touching your source of bliss, then your branches in the outside will flower. In the past the religions have tried to create a split between the outside and the inside—it was a reactionary attitude. Because they saw people, worldly people, too

concerned with the outside, they turned to the opposite pole: they became too concerned, overly concerned, with the inner. But they created a split and that split has been one of the greatest calamities humanity has suffered so far: it has created a schizophrenic humanity.

The outside and the inside look like enemies to each other; the worldly person and the otherworldly person look like enemies. The worldly is the sinner and the otherworldly is the saint.

A seeker has to be both together: in the world and yet not of it, with roots in the inner and flowers in the outer. He hasn't to escape to the Himalayas, to the monasteries; he has to live in the marketplace and yet live silently, peacefully, lovingly, meditatively. That is the only way that we can create a whole human being. And to me, to be whole is to be holy.

The inner is not the only dimension of sacredness; the outer is also the same. But certainly first the roots have to grow, then the branches can follow. If the tree grows first it will fall down, it will not stand.

So the seeker first has to become more and more meditative, more and more blissful, then naturally he starts growing new foliage on the outside, he becomes greener, he rises higher. And when the roots are nourished by the bliss inside, sooner or later the branches are bound to be burdened with flowers. That is the moment a person becomes a buddha . . .

TO BE AWARE IS THE KEY

And in the Beginning You Have to Make an Effort

I can see great possibilities in you, so rather than putting your energies into trivia, direct your energies toward only one thing, and that is how to become more aware, how to become more alert, how to live in a conscious way, deliberately conscious.

In the beginning you have to make an effort to be conscious. Once the effort penetrates and has transformed another chunk of your being, then you can forget about it. It remains conscious. Once it becomes conscious, it remains conscious; it cannot fall back—there is no way to fall back. Then you can work on another chunk of your being, and slowly, slowly, inch by inch, you start penetrating your own palace. And the deeper you go, the more blissful you become. The day your whole being is full of light is a day of rejoicing.

That's what Jesus means when he says, "The Kingdom of God is within you. But be awake," he repeats a thousand and one times: "Be awake, stay awake!"

Once, somebody asked, "What do you mean?" He said, "It is like the man who went on a long journey. He told his servants, 'Stay awake because I can come back anytime and I would not like you to be asleep when I come.' He didn't tell them when he would be coming—tomorrow, the day after tomorrow, this month, next month, this year or the next year. The servants had to be continuously alert because the master could come any moment!" Jesus said, "Like that, God can come any moment into you. Be alert!" In fact, by being alert you send an invitation to God.

By "God" I simply mean all the energy that has already become conscious in existence. I don't mean the Christian God, the one who has created the world—no, all the energy of all the buddhas. Christ is a buddha, so is Muhammad. The energy of all the people who have become enlightened is there in existence and goes on increasing. Each enlightened person pours his being into it; that's what God is. The total consciousness that has already happened in existence—that's what God is.

If you make an effort to become aware, that awareness starts flowing toward you because the same attracts the same. If you are unconscious, then the unconscious flows toward you because the same attracts the same. So just a small effort to become conscious and you will find more is happening than you are making effort for—and that's where you start feeling the help of existence, never otherwise.

When you make a small effort and you see that the result is so much more than the effort made—something plus—then for the first time you become aware that existence is flowing toward you. Your effort brings something, but something more is happening, for which you have not made any effort at all. That's what is called grace. When the ultimate happens it is not mathematically proportionate to your efforts; your efforts are very tiny. You had asked only for a drop and the whole ocean pours into your being.

ONLY ONE STRATEGY

I simply give you one small thing that has to be worked out within your heart—and that is to be more alert. Do whatever you want to do: do it with more consciousness.

Walking on the road, walk more consciously; keep alert that you are walking. Breathing, doing nothing, just breathe, conscious that you are breathing. The breath is going in—be conscious of it. The breath is going out—be conscious of it.

Make every opportunity a device to become more conscious, and soon more and more consciousness will be flowing into you, will be flooding you; more than you were working for. Then you will see the hands of the divine helping you. And once those hands have been seen, trust arises. Then you know that you are not alone.

EXPERIMENT!

You have been searching and seeking for many lives but you have never been persistent; many times you started and stopped. You have tried to dig the well many times but you never went all the way, so you have dug many holes but the water has never come. This time make it a very deliberate effort. Meditation can bring great pleasures, great blessings, but one has to go into it.

The beginning is difficult, and to persevere is the most difficult thing because the mind wavers—one day it will say, "Nothing is happening, why bother?" or "We will do it tomorrow" or "Today there are so many other things to do." The mind always goes on postponing, and meditation needs a continuous effort because it is a very soft phenomenon. It is not like a rock, it is like water falling: if it falls continuously, even rocks will break, but continuity is needed. It is a very soft, feminine energy, so if the continuity remains, by and by everything that comes in its way disappears.

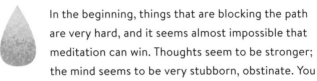

In the beginning, things that are blocking the path are very hard, and it seems almost impossible that meditation can win. Thoughts seem to be stronger; the mind seems to be very stubborn, obstinate. You try to be silent and nothing happens: in fact the moment you try to be silent, more thoughts come. When they see that you are challenging them they give a good fight, and they prove to you that it is not possible, that you should drop the whole effort, the whole project is nonsense. So in the beginning the enemy is very strong, and the friend is very soft and very delicate, almost invisible, intangible, very elusive. The mind tends to surrender to the enemy. But if one can persist, within six to twelve months something simply starts happening. It is only a question of constant effort, time and time again, and not listening to the mind.

Even if nothing is happening, don't be worried. You have been sleeping your whole life and nothing has happened; you have been taking your bath every day and nothing has happened, but still you go on taking a bath: it cleanses, it is good. In just the same way let meditation become part of your ordinary life: one hour has to be given to it—every day. And if one hour can be given to it, within six to twelve months you will see something has started happening that is tremendously valuable. Just do all the meditations, and then you can choose one—whichever feels like it is going deeper, and is in tune with you. And when you have chosen, continue it for at least a year, and much is possible.

Unless your inner and outer become one whole,
you will remain incomplete—and incompletion
is misery. Only in completion is there bliss.
Only in completion have you come home.

You have come to existence without any conflict,
in tremendous ease, relaxed.

AWARE OF WHO YOU ARE
and Where You Are

●●●●●●●●●●●●●●●●●●●●●●●

There is a beautiful story—it looks a little profane, but only Zen Buddhists can do that. They love their master so much, they love Buddha so much, that they can even afford profanity.

There is a story that a monkey came to Buddha—the monkey represents man, the monkey means the mind. The mind is a monkey. Charles Darwin came to know it very, very late—but in the East we have always been aware that man must have come from the monkeys, because he is still monkeyish. Just watch the mind, its constant chattering, and then watch a monkey in the tree. You will feel a similarity.

A monkey came to Buddha, and he was no ordinary monkey. He was a king, a king of monkeys—that means absolutely a monkey! The monkey said to Buddha, "I would like to become a buddha."

Buddha said, "I have never heard of anybody ever becoming a buddha while remaining a monkey."

The monkey said, "You don't know my powers. I am no ordinary monkey." No monkey thinks that he is ordinary, all monkeys think that they are extraordinary; that is part of their monkeyness. He said, "I am no ordinary monkey. What are you talking about? I am a king of monkeys."

So Buddha asked, "What exceptional or extraordinary powers do you have? Can you show me?"

The monkey said, "I can jump to the very end of the world." He had been jumping all along in the trees. He knew how to jump.

So Buddha said, "Okay. Come onto the palm of my hand and jump to the other end of the world."

The monkey tried and tried, and he was really a very powerful monkey, a very intense monkey. He went like an arrow: he went

and he went and he went. Months and—the story says—years passed. And then the monkey came to the very end of the world.

He laughed, and he said, "Look! The very end!" He looked down. It was an abyss: five pillars were standing there to mark the boundary. Now he had to go back, but how would he prove that he had been to these five pillars? So he pissed on a pillar to mark it.

Years passed, and he arrived back. When he reached Buddha he said, "I have been to the very end of the world, and I have left a mark."

But Buddha said, "Just look around."

He had not moved at all. Those five pillars were the five fingers of Buddha, and they were stinking! The monkey had been there with closed eyes—must have been dreaming. The mind is a monkey with closed eyes, dreaming. You have never gone anywhere, you have always been here and now—because nothing else exists. Just open the eyes. Just open the eyes and have a look around, and suddenly you will laugh. You have always been rooted in the ultimate being; there is no need to merge. The only need is to become alert about where you are, who you are.

THE HIDDEN TREASURE

Most people never come to know of their consciousness—it is a hidden treasure. You do not know what it contains unless you awaken it, unless you bring it into the light, unless you open all the doors and enter into your own being, and find every nook and corner. Consciousness in its fullness will give you the idea of who you are, and will also give you the idea of what your destiny is, of where you are supposed to go, of what your capacities are. Are you hiding a poet in your heart, or a singer, or a dancer, or a mystic?

Consciousness is something like light. Right now you are in deep darkness inside. When you close your eyes there is darkness and nothing else.

One of the great philosophers of the West, C. E. M. Joad, was dying, and a friend who was a disciple of George Gurdjieff had come to see him. Joad asked his friend, "What do you go on doing with this strange fellow, George Gurdjieff? Why are you wasting your time? And not only you, I have heard that many people are wasting their time."

His friend laughed. He said, "It is strange that those few people who are with Gurdjieff think that the whole world is wasting its time, and you are thinking that we are wasting our time."

Joad said, "I don't have much longer to live; otherwise I would have come and compared."

The friend said, "Even if you have only a few seconds more to live, it can be done here, now." Joad agreed. The man said, "Close your eyes and just look inside, and then open your eyes and tell me what you find."

Joad closed his eyes, then opened his eyes and said, "There is darkness and nothing else." The friend laughed and he said, "It is not a time to laugh, because you are almost dying, but I have come at the right time. You said that you saw only darkness inside?" Joad said, "Of course."

And the man said, "You are such a great philosopher; you have written such beautiful books. Can't you see the point, that

C. E. M. JOAD

GEORGE GURDJIEFF

there are two things—you and the darkness? Otherwise, who saw the darkness? Darkness cannot see itself—that much is certain—and darkness cannot report that there is only darkness." Joad gave it consideration and he said, "My God, perhaps the people who are with Gurdjieff are not wasting their time. This is true, I have seen the darkness."

His friend said, "Our whole effort is to make this 'I,' the witness, stronger and more crystallized, and to change the darkness into light. And both things happen simultaneously. As the witness becomes more and more centered, the darkness becomes less and less. When the witness comes to its full flowering, that is the lotus of consciousness—all darkness disappears."

Bring more and more crystallization to your witness, to your consciousness; so that your inner being, your interiority, becomes a light, so full and overflowing that you can share it with others.

To be in darkness is to be living at the minimum. And to be full of life is to live at the maximum.

FACE YOUR REALITY

First, a story: There was a little polar bear who asked his mother, "Was my daddy also a polar bear?"

"Of course your daddy was a polar bear."

"But," goes on the little one after a while, "Mommy, just tell me, was my grandfather also a polar bear?"

"Yes, he was also a polar bear."

Time goes by, and the little one keeps asking his mother, "But what about my great-grandfather? Was he a polar bear as well?"

"Yes, he was. But why are you asking?"

"Because I'm freezing!"

A friend has asked: "Osho, I was told my father was a polar bear, I was told my grandfather was a polar bear, I was told my great-grandfather was a polar bear; but I am freezing. How can I change this?"

I happen to know your father, and I happen to know your grandfather, and I happen to know your great-grandfather, too; and they were also freezing. And their mothers told the same story to them: "Your father was a polar bear and your grandfather was a polar bear and your great-grandfather was a polar bear."

If you are freezing, you are freezing; these stories won't help. This simply proves that even polar bears freeze. Look at the reality, and don't move into traditions, and don't go into the past. If you are freezing, you are freezing! And it is not a consolation at all that you are a polar bear.

These consolations have been given to humanity.

A man is dying, and you console him by telling him that the soul is immortal. These consolations are of no help. Somebody is in misery, and you tell him, "Don't be miserable. It is just psychological." How does it help? You make him even more miserable! These theories are not of much help. They have been invented to console, to deceive.

If you are freezing, you are freezing. Rather than asking whether your father was a polar bear, do some exercise. Jump, jog, or do Dynamic Meditation, and you won't freeze, I promise you. Forget all about your father and grandfather and great-grandfather. Just listen to your reality. If you are freezing, then do something. And something can always be done. But this is no way—you are on a wrong track. You can go on asking and asking, and of course your poor mother goes on consoling you.

The question is beautiful, very meaningful, has tremendous import. This is how humanity is suffering. Listen to the suffering; look into the problem. And don't try to find any solutions outside the problem. Look directly into the problem, and you will always find the solution there. Look into the question; don't ask for the answer.

For example, you can go on asking, "Who am I?" You can go to a Christian and he will say, "You are a son of God, and God loves you very much." And you will be puzzled, because how can God love you?

Or you go to the Hindus and ask, and they say, "You are God himself." Not the son of God, you are God himself. But still you have your headache and your migraine, and you are very puzzled at how God can have a migraine—and it doesn't solve the problem.

If you want to ask, "Who am I?" don't go to anybody. Sit silently and ask deeper into your own being. Let the question resound—not verbally, existentially. Let the question be there like an arrow piercing your heart: "Who am I?" And go with the question.

Don't be in a hurry to answer it, because if you answer it, that answer will have come from somebody else—some priest, some politician, some tradition. Don't answer from your memory, because your memory is all borrowed. Your memory is just like a computer, very dead! Your memory has nothing to do with knowing. It has been fed into you.

So when you ask, "Who am I?" and your memory says, "You are a great soul," watch out. Don't fall into the trap. Just discard all this rubbish; it is all rot. Just go on asking, "Who am I? Who am I? Who am I?" and one day you will see that the question, too, has disappeared. There is only a thirst left—"Who am I?" Not the question, really, but a thirst: your whole being throbbing with the thirst—"Who am I?"

And one day you will see you are not even there; there is only thirst. And in that intense, passionate state of your being, suddenly you will realize something has exploded. Suddenly you will have come face-to-face with yourself, and you will know who you are.

There is no way to ask your father, "Who am I?" He himself does not know who he is. There is no way to ask your grandfather or great-grandfather. Don't ask! Don't ask your mother, don't ask society, don't ask the culture, don't ask civilization. Ask your own innermost core. If you really want to come to know the answer, go inward. And from that inward experience, change happens.

You ask, "How can I change this?" You cannot change it. First you have to face your reality, and that very encounter will change you.

THE THREE PRINCIPLES
●●●●●●●●●●●●●●●●●●●●●●●●

Meditation has nothing to do with controlling the mind—because every control is a kind of repression, and that which is repressed will take its revenge. Whenever you relax a little, the mind that was in control will immediately come up and start to stir up everything within you, with vengeance.

Meditation is not control, because control creates tension and meditation is based on relaxation. Meditation has a few essential things in it, whatever the method. But those few essentials are necessary in every method.

The first is a relaxed state: no fight with the mind, no control of the mind, no concentration.

Second, just watching with a relaxed awareness whatever is going on, without any interference. And third: just watching the mind, silently, without any judgment, any evaluation. These are the three things: relaxation, watching, no judgment.

Slowly, slowly a great silence descends over you. All movement within you ceases. You are, but there is no sense of "I am"—just a pure space.

There are one hundred and twelve methods of meditation, and I have talked on all those methods. They differ in their constitution, but the fundamentals remain the same: relaxation, watchfulness, a nonjudgmental attitude.

More methods can be created—I have created many more methods—but just the essential ingredients should be there.

You can change the device according to the times, according to individuals, but you cannot leave out these three things: relaxation, watchfulness, and a nonjudgmental attitude.

So, in fact, just these three things are the only method of meditation; all others are variations of the same theme.

If one meditates with just these three essentials, he can create as many methods for different situations, different people, as he likes. But he should have his own experience.

A QUICK METHOD
Get Tense . . . and Let Go!

WHEN: every evening, before going to sleep
DURATION: 4 to 6 minutes

● ●

Every night before you go to sleep, stand in the middle of the room—exactly in the middle—and make your body as stiff and as tense as possible: almost as if you will burst. Do this for two minutes, and then relax for two minutes, standing up. Do this tensing and relaxing two or three times, and then just go to sleep.

Remember: the whole body has to be made as tense as possible. Afterward, don't do anything else, so the whole night that relaxation goes deeper and deeper in you.

Remember, the first thing in the day sets the trend, and the last thing in the night also sets the trend. So begin your sleep with a deep relaxation, and the whole night becomes *samadhi*, the whole night becomes a deep meditation—relaxed.

Six, seven, or eight hours is a long time. If you live for sixty years, you will be in your bed for twenty years. Twenty years is a long time, and if you can change the quality of your sleep, you need not go to a forest to meditate.

MEDITATION: ABSOLUTE RELAXATION

Meditation is nothing but absolute rest.

How you bring that absolute rest depends on many things. There are a thousand and one methods to create that rest. My own methods are such that first I would like you to become as restless as possible, so nothing is left hanging inside you; restlessness has been thrown out—then move into rest. And then there will be no disturbance; it will be easier.

In Buddha's time, such dynamic methods were not needed. People were simpler, more authentic. They lived more real lives. Now people are living very repressed lives, very unreal. When they don't want to smile, they smile. When they want to be angry, they show compassion. People are false; the whole life pattern is false. The whole culture is like a great falsity. People are just acting, not living. So much hangover, so many incomplete experiences go on being collected, piled up inside their minds.

Just sitting directly in silence won't help. The moment you sit silently, you will see all sorts of things moving inside you. You will feel it almost impossible to be silent. First throw those things out, so you come to a natural state of rest. Real meditation starts only when you are at rest.

All the dynamic meditations are just basic requirements to be fulfilled so that real meditation can happen. Don't treat them as meditations; they are just introductory, just a preface. Only when all activity of the body and mind has ceased can the real meditation begin.

A METHOD

to Get Free of Tensions and Blocks

•••••••••••••••••••••••••••

I am more and more aware of the presence of tensions
in my body that block me and limit my movements.
What can I do?

You carry a very strong armor around you. But it is good that you
are becoming aware. It is just an armor, it is not clinging to you.
You are clinging to it, so when you become aware, you can simply
drop it. The armor is dead. If you don't carry it, it will disappear.
Not only are you carrying it, but you are also nourishing and
feeding it continuously. So you have to watch where you feel
limitations in the body. To someone who has had a strong
experience of the limitations he is encasing himself in, feeling
them especially in the legs, and in the neck, chest, and throat: just
do three things.

The first step: exhale deeply
Walking or sitting, or whenever you
are not doing anything, exhale deeply.
The emphasis should be on exhalation,
not on inhalation. So exhale deeply—
throw out as much air as you can,
exhaling through the mouth. But do

it slowly so it takes time; the longer it takes the better, because
then it goes deeper. When all the air inside the body is thrown

out, then the body inhales. Don't *you* inhale. Exhalation should be slow and deep; inhalation should be fast. This will change the armor near the chest and will change your throat, too.

The second step: run toward life
If you can start running a little it will be helpful. Not many miles, just one mile will do. Just visualize that a load is disappearing from the legs, as if it is falling away. The legs carry armor if your freedom has been restricted too much, if you have been told to do this and not to do that; to be this and not to be that; to go here and not to go there. So start running, and while running, also put more attention on the exhalation. Once you regain your legs and their fluidity, you will have a tremendous energy flow.

The third step: take off your armor
When you go to sleep at night, take off your clothes, and while taking them off, just imagine that you are not only taking off your clothes, you are taking off your armor, too. Actually do it. Take it off and have a good deep breath—and then go to sleep as if unarmored, with nothing on the body and no restriction.

   In three weeks tell me how it is going.

CONNECTING
with the Body and the Breath
●●●●●●●●●●●●●●●●●●●●●●●●

It is something very fundamental to understand that the body is always ready to listen to you—you have never talked with it, you have never made any communication with it. You have been in it, you have used it, but you have never thanked it. It serves you, and serves you as intelligently as possible.

I am experiencing difficulty in concentrating in the meditations, can you suggest something?

The first thing—you should not try to concentrate. Concentration is not going to help you at all. Concentration will create a tension in the mind. Relaxation is going to help, not concentration. There are two types of people: there are people who can be helped by concentration, and there are people who can be helped only through relaxation—and the two processes are different.

In concentration you have to focus your mind on something. That will not be possible for you. Your energy cannot move that

way. In relaxation you have simply to relax, unfocused—it is just the contrary to concentration. So I will give you a method for you to start doing at night.

Just before you go to sleep, sit in your chair. Be comfortable. Comfort is the most essential part of it. For relaxation, one has to be very comfortable. So make yourself comfortable: whatever posture you want to take in the chair, take. Close your eyes and relax the body. Just from the toes up to the head, feel inside where you feel the tension. If you feel it at the knee, relax the knee. Just touch the knee and say to the knee, "Please relax." If you feel tension in the shoulders, just touch the place and say, "Please relax." Within a week you will be able to communicate with your body. And once you start communicating with your body, things become very easy.

The body need not be forced, it can be persuaded. One need not fight with the body—that's ugly, violent, aggressive, and any sort of conflict is going to create more and more tension. So you need not be in any conflict—let comfort be the rule. And the body is such a beautiful gift from existence that to fight with it is to deny existence itself. It is a shrine: we are enshrined in it; it is a temple. We exist in it and we have to take every care of it—it is our responsibility.

So for seven days . . . It will look a little absurd in the beginning because we have never been taught to talk to our own body—and miracles can happen through the body. They are already happening without our knowing it.

So the first thing: relax in the chair; have the light as dark or dim as you like, but the light should not be bright. Tell everybody, "For these twenty minutes no disturbance, no phone call, nothing whatever," as if the world is no more for those twenty minutes. Close the door, relax in the chair with loose clothes so there is no tightness anywhere, and start feeling where the tension is. You will find many spots of tension. Those have to be relaxed first because if the body is not relaxed, the mind cannot be, either. The body creates the situation for the mind to relax. The body becomes the vehicle of relaxation.

Unless the body gives a base, nothing is possible. So the first thing is to create a body base.

Just go on touching the place: wherever you feel some tension, touch your own body with deep love, with compassion. The body is your servant, and you have not paid anything for it—it is simply a gift. And so complicated, so tremendously complex that science has not been able yet to make anything like the body. But we never think about that; we don't love the body. On the contrary, we feel angry about it. And the so-called saints have taught many foolish things to people—that the body is the enemy, that the body is your degradation. That the body is pulling you downward, that the body is a sin; it is all sin.

If you want to commit a sin, the body helps, that's true. But the responsibility is yours, not the body's. If you want to meditate, the body is ready to help you in that, too. If you want to go downward, the body follows you. If you want to go upward, the body follows you. The body is not the culprit at all. The whole responsibility is of your own consciousness—but we always try to find scapegoats. The body has been one of the most ancient scapegoats. You can throw anything at it. And the body is dumb; it cannot retaliate, it cannot answer, it cannot say that you are wrong. So whatever you say, there is no reaction from the body against it.

Go on all over the body and surround it with loving compassion, with deep sympathy, with care. This will take at least five minutes, and you will start feeling very, very limp, relaxed, almost sleepy.

Then bring your consciousness to the breathing: relax the breathing.

The body is our outermost part, the consciousness the innermost, and the breathing is the bridge that joins them together. That's why once breathing disappears, the person is dead—because the bridge is broken: now the body cannot function as your home, your abode.

So when the body is relaxed, just close your eyes and see your breathing; relax that, too. Have a little talk to the breathing: "Please relax. Be natural." You will see that the moment you say, "Please relax," there will be a subtle click. Ordinarily breathing has become very unnatural. We have forgotten how to relax it

because we are so continuously tense that it has become almost habitual for the breathing to remain tense. So just tell it to relax two or three times and then just remain silent.

At this point, with each breath going out, say "One." As the breath goes out, say "One"; when breathing in, don't say anything. Breathe out and say "One"; breathe in and don't say anything. So with each outgoing breath you simply say "One . . . One . . . One." And not only say it but also feel that the whole existence is one, it is a unity. Don't repeat that, just have the feeling—saying "One" will help.

And remember: you should see whether this process disturbs your sleep, because that is possible. If it does, then the meditation can be done two or three hours before sleeping.

So, this is the method: when the breath goes out, say "One." When it is coming in, remain silent. This "One" and the silence will give you a new understanding between the word and wordlessness. This "One" will be the word, and not saying anything will be the wordlessness. This "One" will be part of language and part of the mind, and the wordlessness will not be a part of the mind—it will be a part of no-mind, of the beyond.

You will be moving just between these two, between the finite and the infinite. Between these two shores, your consciousness will continuously move, and there will be a very subtle harmony created.

FIRST STEPS IN THE ART OF WATCHING

Self-consciousness is not consciousness of the self, and there is the problem. Consciousness of the self is totally different; it is not self-consciousness at all. In fact, self-consciousness is a barrier for consciousness of the self. You can try to watch, observe, with a very self-conscious mind: that is not awareness, that is not witnessing, because that will make you tense.

Remember, witnessing is not ego-consciousness. The ego has to be dropped. And you are not to make it a strain. It has to be relaxed; it has to be in a deep let-go.

If you are continuously thinking in terms of the ego, then even your witnessing will become a disease; then your meditation will become a disease, then your religiousness will become a disease. With the ego, everything becomes a disease. The ego is the great inconvenience in your being. It is like a thorn in the flesh; it goes on hurting. It is like a wound.

So what to do? The first thing, when you are trying to watch, is this: concentrate on the object, and don't concentrate on the subject. Start from the object— concentration. Look at the tree, and let the tree be there. Forget yourself completely; you are not needed. Your being there will be a continuous disturbance in the experience of the greenery, of the tree, of the rose. Just let the rose be there. Become completely oblivious of yourself; focus on the rose. Let the rose be there: no subject, just the object. This is the first step.

Then the second step: drop the rose; drop the emphasis on the rose. Now emphasize the consciousness of the rose—but still no subject is needed, just the consciousness that you are watching, that there is watching.

And only then can the third step be taken, which will bring you close to what Gurdjieff calls self-remembering, or Krishnamurti calls awareness, or the Upanishads call witnessing.

But first the two steps have to be fulfilled; then the third comes easily. Don't start doing the third immediately: first the object, then the consciousness, then the subject.

Once the object is dropped and the emphasis on the consciousness is no longer a strain, the subject is there but there is no subjectivity in it. You are there, but there is no "I" in it, just being. You *are*, but there is no feeling that "I am." That confinement of "I" has disappeared; only "amness" exists. That amness is divine. Drop the "I" and just be that amness.

And if you have been working too long on witnessing, then for a few months—at least for three months—drop it completely, don't do anything about it. Otherwise the old pattern may continue and may pollute the new awareness. For three months give a gap, and for three months meditate with cathartic methods—Dynamic, Kundalini, Nataraj—the type in which the

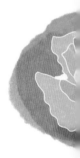

whole emphasis is on doing something, and that something is more important. Just dancing, and the dance becomes important, not the dancer. The dancer has to lose himself completely in dancing. So, for three months, drop witnessing and be absorbed in some meditation. This is totally different; being absorbed in something is completely forgetting yourself. Dancing will be very good, singing will be very good—forget yourself completely in it. Don't keep yourself apart and divided. If you can dance in such a way that only the dance remains and the dancer disappears, one day suddenly you will see the dancing has also disappeared. And then there is an awareness that is not of the mind and not of the ego. In fact, that awareness cannot be practiced; something else has to be done as a preparation, and then the awareness comes to you. You have to just become available for it.

THE METHOD
OSHO Nataraj Meditation

Nataraj is the energy of dance. This is dance as a total meditation, where all inner division disappears and a subtle, relaxed awareness remains.

This meditation is to be done with its specific OSHO Nataraj Meditation music, which indicates and energetically supports the different stages. For further details, see the "Follow-Up" section at the back of the book.

· ·

The meditation lasts 65 minutes and has three stages.

FIRST STAGE: **40 minutes**
With eyes closed, dance as if possessed. Let your unconscious take over completely. Do not control your movements or be a witness to what is happening. Just be totally in the dance.

SECOND STAGE: **20 minutes**
Keeping your eyes closed, lie down immediately. Be silent and still.

THIRD STAGE: **5 minutes**
Dance in celebration and enjoy.

· ·

AWAKENING THE SENSES—SEEING

If you really want to know what the truth is, the scriptures won't help. Neither will going to the Himalayas be of any help. Only one thing can help: start looking at things without the mind. Look at the flower and don't allow the mind to say anything. Just look at it. It is difficult because of an old habit of interpreting. You go on interpreting, and interpretations differ. Interpretations depend on the mind.

How you look at things depends on you, not on things. Unless you come to a point where you drop the interpreting mind and look directly, look immediately, mind is your mediator. It brings you things distorted; it brings you things mixed with interpretations. They are not pure.

So the only way to reach truth is in learning how to be immediate in your vision, how to drop the help of the mind. This agency of the mind is the problem, because mind can create only dreams. But mind can create beautiful dreams, and you can get so excited. Through your excitement the dream starts looking like reality.

If you are too excited then you are intoxicated, then you are not in your senses. Then whatever you see is just your projection. And there are as many worlds as there are minds, because every mind lives in its own world. You can laugh at others' foolishnesses, but unless you start laughing at your own, you will not be able to become a man of Tao, a man of nature, a man of truth. So what to do?

Try in small things not to bring the mind in. You look at a flower—simply look. Don't say, "Beautiful! Ugly!" Don't say anything. Don't bring words, don't verbalize. Simply look. The mind will feel uncomfortable, uneasy. The mind would like to say something. Simply say to the mind, "Be silent! Let me see. I will just look."

In the beginning it will be difficult, but start with things in which you are not too much involved. It will be difficult to look at your wife without bringing words in. You are too much involved, too much emotionally attached. Angry or in love, but too much involved.

Look at things that are neutral—a rock, a flower, a tree, the sun rising, a bird in flight, a cloud moving in the sky. Just look at things with which you are not much involved, with which you can remain detached, with which you can remain indifferent. Start from neutral things, and only then move toward emotionally loaded situations.

People start from the loaded situations; they fail, because it is almost impossible. Either you love your wife or you hate, there is no in between. If you love you are mad, if you hate you are

mad—and both ways the words will come. It is almost impossible not to allow the words, difficult because of so much practice in continuously saying something. Awake, or even in sleep, when you are emotionally too much involved, it is difficult to put the mind aside. It will come in. So look at unloaded situations first. When you have the feeling that, yes, you can look at certain things without the mind coming in, then try with loaded relationships.

By and by, one becomes efficient. It is just like swimming: in the beginning you feel afraid, and in the beginning you cannot imagine how you will survive. And you have been working with the mind so long, you cannot think that without the mind you can exist for a single moment. But try!

And the more you put the mind aside, the more light will happen to you, because when there are no dreams, doors are open, windows are open, and the sky reaches to you, and the sun rises and it comes to the very heart; the light reaches you.

You become more and more filled with truth as you are less and less filled with dreaming.

IDENTIFICATION
the basic problem

●●●●●●●●●●●●●●●●●●●●●●●

Things go on changing without.
You must mirror them,
you must reflect them,
but remember always that the mirror remains the same.
Mirroring does not change the mirror.
Do not be identified with mirroring.
Remember yourself as the mirror—
that is what is meant by witnessing.
And witnessing is meditation.

Lieh-Tzu exhibited his skill in archery to Po-Hun Wu-Jen. When the bow was drawn to its full length, a cup of water was placed on his elbow and he began to shoot. As soon as the first arrow was let fly, a second one was already on the string, and a third followed.

In the meantime he stood unmoved like a statue.

Po-Hun Wu-Jen said: "The technique of your shooting is fine, but it is still a technique. You look just like a statue from without. Now let us go up to a high mountain and stand on a rock projecting over a precipice, and then you try to shoot."

They climbed up a mountain. Standing on a rock projecting over a precipice ten thousand feet high Po-Hun Wu-Jen stepped backward until one third of his feet was hanging over the rock.

He then motioned to Lieh-Tzu to come forward. Lieh-Tzu fell to the ground with perspiration running down to his heels.

Po-Hun Wu-Jen said: "The perfect man soars up above the blue sky or dives down to the yellow springs, or wanders about all over the eight limits of the world, yet shows no signs of change in his spirit. But you betray a sign of trepidation and your eyes are dazed. How can you expect to hit the target?"

THE METHOD

Find Your Meditation

● ●

Anything that leads you to yourself is meditation. And it is immensely significant to find your own meditation, because in the very finding you will find great joy. And because it is your own finding—not some ritual imposed upon you—you will love to go deeper into it. The deeper you go into it, the happier you will feel—peaceful, more silent, more together, more dignified, more graceful.

You all know watching, so there is no question of learning it. It is just a question of changing the object of watching. Bring them closer.

Watch your body, and you will be surprised. I can move my hand without watching, and I can move my hand with watching. You will not see the difference, but I can feel the difference. When I move it with watchfulness, there is a grace and beauty in it, a peacefulness, and a silence. You can walk, watching each step; it will give you all the benefit that walking can give you as an exercise, plus it will give you the benefit of a great, simple meditation.

NATURE HAS TO BECOME
Your Meditation
●●●●●●●●●●●●●●●●●●●●●●●●●

Think of these things: the snow-capped peaks of the mountains, the sunlit peaks of the mountains, the virgin silence of the mountains, the sound of running water and the song of the winds in the trees. Think of these things, because they will remind you of God. *Contemplate these things.*

One of the greatest problems that man is facing is his own man-made world. Now he is surrounded by his own creations—buildings, roads, technology, all that he has made—and they are of immense value, I am all for them, but they don't remind him of God; they can't. On the contrary they remind him only of his own ego, that he is the doer, that he has done all this. And slowly, slowly man is losing contact with nature, and nature is the temple of God.

If you see a painting it reminds you of the painter. If you listen to music it reminds you of the musician.

Nature has to become your meditation. Go to the river, sit by the side of a tree, a rosebush, and be utterly open to nature—

available. Slowly, slowly a great remembrance starts arising in one's being. God is not lost, only forgotten, so all that is needed is not a search for God but a remembrance. From where to get the remembrance? Watch life, growing things, trees . . .

The building made of cement and concrete does not grow. It has no life—it is dead from the very beginning. Think of things that grow, because God is nothing but the growing principle of existence. God is the evolution in existence, that constant growing. And the most important thing in life is to understand what growth is. The really religious person is one who becomes intrigued with this mysterious phenomenon called growth.

A seed becomes a sprout and it goes on growing. This is the greatest miracle that is happening every day. A woman becomes pregnant and life starts growing. Wherever there is growth, there is life, and wherever there is life there is God; God is another name for life. Whenever you can find time, come closer to nature, have more and more contact with nature, and that will become your meditation. And even in imagination it will be of immense help. Falling asleep, think of the mountains, falling asleep be with the mountains. Go on falling into sleep remembering the rivers and the trees and the roses, and soon you will be able to see a change happening in your sleep, too: it will become God-full!

To be constantly in contact with nature is the only way to remember God—all other ways are just poor substitutes.

THE METHOD

Opening the Heart

● ●

To open your heart you need not do anything in particular, because the heart is a very indirect, delicate phenomenon. If you start doing something to open it, that very doing will close it. It will be like forcing the petals of a rose flower to open. That won't help; it will destroy the flower.

One cannot be direct about the heart, one has to be indirect. One has to be very, very delicate about it—not gross, very subtle. Listen to music. Go into nature whenever you can find time: be with the trees, birds, animals. Look at the stars in the night. Sing, dance. These are indirect ways—you are not doing anything directly to open the heart. Be loving, be friendly, even with strangers. These are all indirect ways. This is how one can nourish the opening heart.

So go on becoming more and more sensitive and do whatever helps in becoming more sensitive, but don't be direct: dance, sing, play music.

BECOME LOVE, BECOME LIGHT

Reality is a net of love and light rays, a synthesis of love and light.

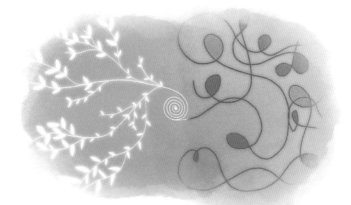

If you go through a scientific approach, you will find nothing but light, a network of light and rays. If you go through religion, you will find a network of love energy.

Life is one—it can be interpreted in two ways: either as light or as love. It depends on your method of approach. If the approach is scientific, you will come to the ultimate stratum of reality as light. If the approach is of the heart—not of logic, but of intuition; not of reason, but irrational . . . If the approach is that of prayer and not calculation, you will stumble upon the same reality; reality is one, but now your interpretation will be that of love. And it is better to understand it in both ways; then you have a total concept, and the vision is perfect.

Try to understand from both sides. Sometimes approach your inner reality as a phenomenon of light: just think of yourself as nothing but light. And sometimes approach your innermost door as love. When you are alone, think of yourself as light; when you are with somebody, think of yourself as love. When you are alone, enter your reality with the meditation that you are light.

When you are alone, become light—that is the way of meditation. When you relate with people, become love—that is the way of prayer. And try to catch hold of your reality from both ways. Either one way is lopsided. And there is no need to miss the other, because the other is also tremendously beautiful. Just to feel oneself as light—as infinite crisscrossing waves of light, rays of light; just a net, a beautiful net of nothing but light—is so incredibly beautiful. It's fantastic.

Many people come to reality through this experience. But this is half, one aspect of the truth. And if one remains confined to it, something is missing. This type of man will become very detached. He will not relate. He will become an escapist; he will avoid relationships. In fact, he will become afraid of relationships because whenever he is in a relationship, that incredible experience of light will disappear.

It happens only when you are alone: tremendously alone, unrelated—only then does it happen. It is a nonrelating experience. Because of this experience, Buddhists, Jainas, all became escapists and renounced the world. *Love* became a dangerous word. The same happened in Christianity, too. It should not have happened there, because Jesus goes on saying that God is love—still it happened!

The human mind tends to choose. It is very difficult to choose the whole, because to choose the whole means to be choiceless, and the human mind tends to choose one aspect of it. Once you choose one aspect, the other is denied. And then you become afraid of the other, because if the other comes in, your first experience will be disturbed. So you become protective.

Sufis, *bhaktas*, devotees, have experienced the other aspect of reality through love, prayer, feelings, the heart—but they become afraid of the light because light disturbs their love, their relationships. And my whole effort is to create the ultimate synthesis, so you are capable of knowing reality in as many ways as it is.

Don't become obsessed with any partial view. Remain available. Even to the opposite, remain available; even to the contradictory, remain available. If one is available to contradictions and can easily float from one to the other, the mind disappears utterly, because the mind cannot exist with a choiceless awareness. So don't choose between these two.

When you relate with people, become love. When you are alone, become light. Go on playing with both the ideas, and soon you will see a synthesis arising. And that synthesis is what life is: a synthesis of light and love.

These three L's are the most important: love, light, life. Just as there are three R's in the world of learning, there are three L's in the world of unlearning: love, light, life.

THE METHOD
Be Full of Loving Energy

● ●

Consider this method as a process on yourself: Just dissolve yourself into a loving energy, just become a loving energy—not in love with something in particular, but just having love for each and everything . . . even for nothing! It is not a question of an object of love but of just an overflowing loving energy.

If you are sitting silently in your room, let the room be full of loving energy; create an aura of love around yourself. And you *can* do it; that's why I am saying it. I only give things to you that I can see are possible. I don't ask the impossible—never! I only indicate what is going to happen to you very naturally. It is very

simple and very naturally possible for you to become just love. That will be your prayer, and that will be your meditation.

If you are looking at the trees, you are in love with the trees; if you are looking at the stars, you are in love with the stars. You are love, that's all. So wherever you are, go on pouring your love: onto rocks, and when you pour love on rocks, even rocks are no longer rocks. Love is such a miracle, such magic, that it transforms everything into the beloved. You become love and existence becomes your beloved, existence becomes God.

People seek and search for God without becoming love. How can they find God? They don't have the necessary equipment, the necessary context and space. Create love and forget all about God. Suddenly one day you will encounter godliness everywhere.

ACCEPT YOURSELF . . .
and Relax in Your Totality!

The whole purpose of all religious endeavor is to create a state of peace within you. Ordinarily man is constantly in turmoil, in inner conflict, in a kind of civil war, and the war goes on and on. It destroys your whole life because it dissipates your energy. This war has to be stopped.

The so-called organized religions have not been helpful; on the contrary, they have created more and more of this inner conflict. They have made it more acute, more chronic, more of a cancer, because they create guilt. They divide every human being into the lower and the higher, into the good and the bad. And once you are divided, you are bound to be in struggle—a struggle with yourself. You cannot win, and you cannot be defeated, either. You remain in limbo, fighting and fighting: no defeat, no victory; nothing comes out of it—simply frustration, boredom. That's what has happened to the whole of humanity.

This is not the way of the buddhas. The buddha may be Gautam Siddhartha or Jesus Christ or Zarathustra or Lao Tzu—it doesn't matter who the awakened one is, but this is the way of all the awakened ones: not to create conflict in you.

And this is my way, too: I want you to love yourself, because only through that love does peace descend. I want you to accept yourself in toto, as you are. Not that that means there will be no growth: in fact, once you accept yourself as you are, a great explosion happens, because the energy that gets involved in conflict is released and that energy is available for you. That makes you strong, that makes you more intelligent, that makes you more alert, that makes you more alive; that creates a soul in you.

So this is your first lesson: accept yourself, love yourself. Drop all guilt, don't divide yourself. There is nothing higher, nothing lower; all of you is divine. The lowest is as divine as the highest. Matter is as divine as consciousness. Matter is one aspect of God, consciousness another aspect. There is no question of lower and higher; there is no question of hierarchy.

Just by understanding it, you suddenly see great peace settling inside. And with that peace is the beginning of a radical change, of a revolution, of a new birth.

THE METHOD

Relax Before Going to Sleep

"I feel a certain restlessness, particularly in my arms.
It feels as if I need to do something energetic.
What can I do to settle this restlessness?"

Every night, sit in a chair and rest your head, as you do in a
dentist's chair. You can use a pillow, so you are in a resting
posture. Then release your lower jaw, just relax it so the mouth
opens slightly, and start breathing from the mouth, not from the
nose. But the breathing has not to be changed, it has to be just
as it is—natural. The first few breaths will become a little hectic.
By and by it will settle down and the breathing will become very
shallow. It will go in and out very slightly; that's how it should be.
Keep the mouth open, eyes closed, and rest. Then start feeling
that your legs are becoming loose, as if they are being taken away
from you, broken at the joints. Feel as if they are being taken

away from you, they have been cut loose, broken off, and then start thinking that you are just the upper part: the legs are gone.

Then the hands: think that both the hands are becoming loose and being taken away from you. You may even be able to hear a click inside when they are broken off. You are no longer your hands—they are dead, taken away. Just the torso remains. Then start thinking about the head—it is being taken away, you are being beheaded, the head is broken off. Leave it loose: wherever it turns—right, left—you cannot do anything. Just leave it loose; it has been taken away. Then you have just your torso.

Feel that you are only this much—the chest, the belly, that's all. Do this for at least twenty minutes, and then go to sleep. This is to be done just before sleep, for at least three weeks.

It is just that your body is not aligned; the energy is not proportionately distributed. Taking each part as separate, only the essential will remain, so your whole energy will move within the essential part. That essential part will relax, and the energy will start flowing again in your legs, in your hands, in your head, in a more proportionate way. A new distribution of energies is needed. It is always energy being more in one part, less in another, that makes you feel lopsided. So your hands must be getting more energy than other parts. Then you want to do something with your hands, and if you cannot find anything to do, you can become angry. The hands get angry if they have too much energy: when they cannot do anything, they want to destroy. Either they create or they destroy. If you can create, good; if you cannot create, then destruction. So just do this for three weeks.

A GOOD USE OF BREATHING

"How is one to watch the breath when it is
not seen but felt?"

Watching need not be seeing, it can be feeling. In fact it has to
be a feeling because how can you see your breath? You feel it,
the touch of it. When the breath moves through the passage,
you feel the touch of it. The whole thing is not a question of
seeing.

The thing is to be alert that it is going in, that it has
reached the very innermost core of your being; that now it
has stopped; that now it is coming back. The ebb and the flow:
now it has gone out, moved completely out, stopped; then
again moving back. The whole circle of it—coming in, going out,
coming in, going out—one has to be aware. If you feel it, that is
awareness—but one should not miss feeling it. If you can do it
every day for an hour, your whole life will be changed.

Remember, if you don't change your breathing there is
no chemical change happening in you. That's the difference
between Patanjali and Buddha. Patanjali's yoga techniques
will change your chemistry; Buddha's technique will not touch
your chemistry at all. Normal breathing—as it is: you simply
watch, feel, see. Don't let it go in and out without awareness,
that's all. Don't change it. Let it be as it is. Just add one thing:
that you remain a witness to it.

Even if you can do it for one hour, your whole life will be transfigured—and without any chemical change. You will simply become a transcendental experience, a transcendental consciousness. You will not see Buddhas, you will become a buddha. And that's the point to be remembered: seeing Buddhas does not matter . . . unless you become a buddha.

A METHOD

to Deal with Chaos and Confusion

•••••••••••••••••••••••••

"Since I started meditating, the confusion in me has
largely increased. What is happening?"

It is a good sign. Something is happening—only then does one get mixed up, confused, otherwise not. If you just go on living the way you have always lived you have a clarity—not the clarity that I talk about, but you have a certain clarity. You go on following the old habits, the same pattern, and you move smoothly.

When you come in contact with a person like me, and if the contact really happens, you will feel confused and mixed up because the new will start happening and the old is still there. You will be hesitating, wavering as to whether to continue with the old or take a jump into the new. Everything will become a chaos— that's a good sign.

My whole effort is to help you to come to such a critical point where you have to decide either for the future and gamble with the whole past, or to completely close off the future and move with the comfort and convenience of the past.

That's why you are feeling mixed up. So don't feel in a hurry to settle things. Allow this confusion to go to the very roots of your being so that you are divided, clearly cut into two parts. In the beginning it will feel almost as if you are becoming schizophrenic, becoming split, but this split is needed. Once you have decided to get out of the past, the confusion will disappear, and clarity will come.

Simply wait, watch. Let the confusion be there. Don't try to sort things out, don't try to figure things out, because whatever you do is not going to help now. Simply watch. This is a great parting of the ways. The way you have walked up to now is no longer going to be your way in the future. You have come to a crossroads. A great decision, a moment of decision is bound to create much turmoil. Simply watch. There is no need to do anything now.

You can do this meditation for fifteen days, every night before you go to sleep:

The first step
Just sit on your bed—sit in a relaxed way—and close your eyes. Feel the body relaxing. If the body starts leaning forward, allow it; it may lean forward. It may like to take a womb posture—just as when a child is in the mother's womb. If you feel like that, just move into the womb posture: become a small child in the mother's womb.

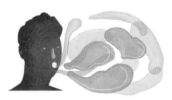

The second step
Just listen to your breathing, nothing else. Just listen to it—the breathing going in, the breathing going out; the breathing going in, the breathing going out. I'm not saying to say it—just feel it going in; when it is going out, feel it going out. Just

feel it, and in that feeling you will feel tremendous silence, and clarity arising.

This is just for ten to twenty minutes—minimum ten, maximum twenty—and then go to sleep.

Practice this for fifteen days.

And about your confusion, remember: just let things happen as if you are not the doer. For fifteen days become completely dead to it. That will be necessary for the fruit to ripen and to fall on its own accord. So don't make any effort to fix it or do anything about it. Just be dead to this confusion.

EMPTYING THE GARBAGE OF THE MIND

If you want to find relaxation, first you have to go through a cathartic process. One of these processes is gibberish.

You may not know from where this word *gibberish* comes from. It comes from a Sufi mystic whose name was Jabbar—and that was his only meditation. Whoever would come, he would say, "Sit down and start!" and people knew what he meant. He never talked; he never gave any discourses. He simply taught people gibberish. Once in a while he would give an example: for half an hour he would talk all kinds of nonsense, in nobody knows

what language. It was not a language; he just uttered nonsense. Still he had thousands of disciples because what he was saying was, "Your mind is nothing but gibberish. Put it aside and you will have a taste of your own being." But Jabbar helped many people to become utterly silent. How long can you go on? The mind becomes empty: slowly, slowly a deep nothingness, and in that nothingness a flame of awareness. It is always present, surrounded by your gibberish. The gibberish has to be taken out; that is your poison.

THE METHOD
Throw Out the Tensions of the Mind

● ●

To use gibberish, don't say things that are meaningful, don't use the language that you know. Use Chinese, if you don't know Chinese. Use Japanese, if you don't know Japanese. Don't use German if you know German. For the first time have a freedom—the same as all the birds have. Simply allow whatever comes to your mind without bothering about its rationality, reasonability, meaning, significance—just the way the birds are doing. Leave all language and the mind aside.

Sit silently in your room and start talking to the walls, but don't torture people. Start talking to the walls—do gibberish.

Gibberish should be taught to everyone. The world will become saner if you can simply sit in your room and talk loudly to nobody in particular for one hour. In the beginning it will look crazy—it is! But it will relieve you of much heat and steam, and after one hour you will feel tremendously quiet.

And it is inhuman to force your gibberish on other people—because you can force it on them. Then they are in trouble, then whatever you have said to them goes on rumbling inside their head,

they have to search for somebody else, and on and on. This way the problem that could have been solved becomes a world problem! You may be gone, but the gibberish that you have put in other people's heads will go on and on for centuries! There is no way to end it; then a full point cannot be put on it.

If you want to throw out your junk, please make it a point not to throw it on any other human being. People have their own already, and it is so much; don't add to it.

But you can go to the river and talk to the river. The river won't listen, so there is no problem: the river won't go mad. You can go to a tree and talk to the tree, and you can talk to the stars, and you can talk to the walls; and that's perfectly good. And if you feel it is too crazy, then write it down, make a diary, and write down everything that you want.

You have to get rid of your steam, but it should not enter anybody else's being; otherwise you are violent. And if people learn this simple thing, the world will become saner.

A LAUGHING MEDITATION
to Wake You Up

When you laugh, laugh through your whole body. You can laugh only with the lips, you can laugh with the throat; that is not going to be very deep.

You can laugh with the lips and the throat, you can make noise that sounds like laughter, but it will not be, and it will not be of much help. It will again be a mechanical act.

When you start laughing remember that you are a small child. Visualize yourself as a small child. When small children laugh, they start rolling on the floor. If you feel like it, start rolling. The whole thing is to get totally involved in it. The noise is not as meaningful as the involvement. And once it starts, you will know.

For two to three days you may not be able to feel whether it is happening or not, but it is going to happen. Bring it from the very roots—just as a flower comes to a tree: it travels from the very roots. By and by it comes up. You cannot see it anywhere else. Only when it comes up and flowers on top can you see it. But it is coming from the roots, from very deep underground. It has traveled up from the depths.

In exactly the same way, laughter should start from the feet and then move upward.

THE METHOD
Laugh with Totality

● ●

WHEN: The first thing in the morning and last
thing in the night before going to sleep.
WHERE: Sit on the floor or on the bed.
DURATION: Just ten minutes are enough.

It is good if it can be made a regular process for ten days.

Also, in the whole day, whenever there is an opportunity,
don't miss—laugh!

Sit on the floor or on the bed and feel as if laughter is coming
from the very soles of your feet.

First close your eyes, and then feel that ripples of laughter
are coming from your feet. They are very subtle. Then they come
to the belly and become more visible; the belly starts shaking and
trembling. Then bring them to the heart, and the heart feels so
full. Then bring it to the throat and then to the lips.

Laughter should start from the feet and move upward. Allow
the whole body to be shaken by it. Feel the trembling vibration,
and cooperate with that vibration. Don't remain stiff—relax.
Cooperate with it. Even if in the beginning you exaggerate it a
little, it will be helpful. If you feel that the hand is shaking, help it
to shake more so the energy starts rippling, streaming. Then start
rolling and laughing.

This is in the night before you go to sleep. Just ten minutes will do, and then fall asleep. Again in the morning, first thing—you can do it in your bed. So, the last thing at night and the first thing in the morning.

The night laughter will set a trend in your sleep. Your dreams will become more joyous, more uproarious, and they will help your morning laughter; they will create the background. The morning laughter will set the trend for the whole day. Whatever you do in the morning, first thing—whatever it is—sets the trend for the whole day.

If you become angry first thing, that becomes a chain. One anger leads to another anger, then another anger leads to another. You feel very vulnerable; any small thing gives you a feeling of being hurt, it feels insulting. One thing leads to another. Laughter is really the best thing to start with, but let it be a whole thing.

In the whole day, whenever there is an opportunity, don't miss—laugh.

LIVING PLAYFULLY

●●●●●●●●●●●●●●●●●●●●●●

Taking things easily and without forcing,
after some time the rush of thought,
outward and inward,
subsides naturally,
and the true face shows itself.
—Bukko, a Zen master

Bukko has come to the ultimate expression of the experience of one's own being. Very rarely has a master succeeded to such a point as Bukko has in his statements.

This is what I have been telling you: to be a buddha is not a difficult job. It is not some achievement for which you need a Nobel Prize. It is the easiest thing in the world, because it has already happened without your knowing.

The buddha is already breathing in you. Just a little recognition, just a little turning inward—and it has not to be done forcibly. If you do it forcibly, you will miss the point. It is very delicate. You have to look inward playfully, not seriously. That's what he means by "taking things easily." Don't take anything seriously.

Existence is very easy. You have got your life without any effort, you are living your life without any effort. You are breathing perfectly well without being reminded; your heartbeat continues even in your sleep—existence is so easy with you! But you are not so easy with existence. You are very close-fisted. You want everything to be turned into an achievement.

Enlightenment cannot be an achievement. How can that which you have already be an achievement? The authentic master simply takes away things that you don't have and you believe you have, and he gives you that which you already have. You have many things that you don't have at all; you just believe that you have them. The master's function is that of a surgeon, to cut out all that is not you and leave behind just the essential core—the eternal being.

It is a very easy phenomenon: you can do it on your own. There is no problem and no risk in taking things easily, but people take things very tensely. They take things very seriously, and that spoils the whole game.

And remember, life is a game. Once you understand it as a game, a deep playfulness arises on its own accord. The victory is not the point; the point is to play totally, joyously, dancingly.

THE METHOD
Moments of Unconscious Meditation

•••••••••••••••••••••••••

In the past, the input volume was one-tenth of one's time and the meditative time was nine-tenths. Now just the reverse is the case: nine-tenths input time and one-tenth meditative time. Very rarely do you relax; very rarely do you just sit silently, doing nothing. Even that one-tenth time of unconscious meditation is disappearing. Once that happens, man will be utterly mad. And that is happening.

What do I mean by unconscious meditative time? You simply go into the garden, you play around with your children—that is unconscious meditative time. Or you swim in the swimming pool—that is unconscious meditative time. Or you mow your lawn, or you listen to the birds—that is unconscious meditative time. That too is disappearing because whenever people have time, they are sitting before their TVs, glued to their seats.

Now, tremendously dangerous information is being put into your mind by the TV; you will not be able to digest it. Or you are reading newspapers—all kinds of nonsense are being fed to you. Whenever you have time you put the radio or the TV on. Or someday you are feeling very good and you want to relax and you go to the movies. What kind of relaxation is this? The movie will not allow you relaxation because information is continuously thrown into you.

Relaxation means no information is thrown into you.

Listening to the call of a bird will do, because no information is fed to you. Listening to music will do, because no information is thrown into you—music that has no language, that is pure sound. It does not give any message; it simply delights you. Dancing will be good, music will be good, working in the garden will be good, playing with children will be good, or just sitting doing nothing will be good. This is the cure for the epidemic of neurosis. And if you do it consciously, the impact will be greater. Create a balance.

ROOTS AND WINGS
●●●●●●●●●●●●●●●●●●●●●●●

Child waiting earthbound.
Cloud sparrow
higher and higher.
—Sampu

It is a small haiku.

It says: *Child waiting earthbound . . .* A child in the mother's womb is waiting to come to the earth. First one has to get roots into the earth; only then can you spread your branches into the sky like wings. Unless you have roots, you cannot spread your wings into the sky. The deeper the roots, the higher goes the tree—almost reaching to the stars.

Only one painter in the West, Vincent van Gogh, had such tremendous insight—almost the insight of a mystic, very close to being a buddha. He always painted his trees surpassing the stars.

He was asked, "What are you doing? This is simply insane. No tree can reach beyond the stars!"

Van Gogh was asked again and again, "Are you mad?" But he said, "I have been sitting by the side of the trees, listening where they are going, and I have always heard that the trees are our earth's ambition to reach the stars. My paintings are not factual, they are poetic. They are the ambitions of the earth to reach the stars."

Sampu is saying, "Child waiting in the mother's womb . . ." For what?—earthbound, he wants to get to the earth, to get his roots

deep into the earth, because unless you have roots in the earth you cannot rise into the sky, you cannot be a cedar of Lebanon, four hundred feet high. Then you need four-hundred-foot-deep roots. A balance is needed; otherwise the tree will fall.

This is one of my basic and essential approaches, that unless you are deeply rooted in materialism you cannot rise into spirituality.

The East has committed one mistake: it has been trying to reach the stars without going deeper into the earth, and it has been a complete failure. The West has committed another mistake: it goes on growing the roots into the earth, into matter, and it has forgotten completely about the stars.

Hence my continuous emphasis that every one of you has to be a Zorba the Buddha. Zorba is the roots in the earth, and the buddha is a longing to fly into ultimate freedom, to reach to the space that is unbounded.

> Child waiting earthbound.
> Cloud sparrow
> higher and higher.

. . . And a bird, a cloud sparrow, goes on higher and higher into the sky. Both need a great synthesis.

Our world is suffering because we have not been able to create a synthesis between East and West, between earth and sky, between spirit and matter, between your inner and the outer. Unless this great synthesis is achieved, humanity has no hope.

THE STRATEGY
Create a Dynamic Balance

Neurosis has never been so epidemic in the past as it is now. It is almost becoming a normal state of the human mind. It has to be understood.

Neurosis is an unbalanced state of mind: too much activity and no inactivity at all, too much masculine and no feminine at all, too much yang and too little of yin. You have to be fifty-fifty, you have to keep a deep balance. A symmetry is needed inside you. You have to be half man, half woman; then you will never be neurotic.

The individual is neither male nor female; it is simple unity. Strive to achieve this unity between time spent doing and time spent not doing. This is wholeness, this is what Buddha called his middle way. Just be exactly in the middle. Remember, you can become unbalanced to either extreme: you can become too active, or you can become too inactive. That has its own pitfalls and dangers. If you become too inactive, your life loses dance, your life loses joy, you start to die. So I am not saying become inactive; I am saying let there be a balance between action and inaction. Let them balance each other, and you be just in the middle. Let them be two wings of your being. No wing should be bigger than the other.

In the West, action has become too big, inaction has disappeared. In the East, inaction became too big and action disappeared. The West knows affluence, richness on the outside, and poverty inside; the East knows richness, affluence inside, and poverty on the outside. Both are in misery because both have chosen extremes.

My approach is neither Eastern nor Western, my approach is neither male nor female; my approach is neither of action nor inaction. My approach is that of utter balance, symmetry in you. Hence I say to the seekers of truth: don't leave the world; be in the world and yet be not of it. This is what Taoists call *wu wei wu*, action through inaction. The meeting of yin and yang, anima and animus—it brings enlightenment. Imbalance is neurosis, balance is enlightenment.

AWAKENING THE SENSES—LISTENING

The mind has created buffers to protect itself because, without your knowing, you are continuously bombarded with thought waves from all around you. Everybody sitting by your side is throwing thought waves toward you; everybody is a broadcasting station. You don't hear it, the person does not shout it, but those waves are carrying his thoughts toward you. So many times you have found yourself puzzling: suddenly a thought has come to you and there seems to be no reason why it should come at this moment. It may not be your thought at all; it may be just the thought of the person who is sitting by your side.

It is just like sound waves carrying messages. They are passing right now, but you don't hear them; but if you just add a small receiver device, you can hear.

To protect itself, each mind has created a subtle wall of buffers so those thoughts are turned back, they don't enter your mind. It is basically good, but then slowly those buffers have grown so much that now they don't allow anything in. Even if you want them to allow something, they are no longer in your control. The only way to break that control is in the same way as breaking your own thoughts: just become a witness of your thoughts. And as your thoughts start disappearing, the need for the buffers to protect those thoughts will not be there; those buffers will start falling away. These are all abstract phenomena, so you cannot see them—but their effects are there. Only one who knows how to meditate is one who knows how to listen, or vice versa. One who knows how to listen knows how to meditate, because it is the same thing.

THE METHOD
Develop the Art of Listening

You just have to understand the strategy.

You can sit by the side of a tree, or on your bed, anywhere—just try to listen to the traffic noise, but intensely and totally, with no judgment that it is good or bad.

Your thoughts will drop, and with that, your buffers will drop—and suddenly a gap opens up that leads you into silence and peace.

For centuries this has been the only way for anyone to come close to the reality of his own being and the mystery of existence. And as you come closer you start feeling cooler, you start feeling happier, you start feeling fulfilled, contented, blissful. A point comes where you are so full of bliss that you can share with the whole world, and still your blissfulness will remain the same.

First you can learn the method; then you have to use that method whenever you can, wherever you can.

And you have so much time—waiting for a bus, sitting in a train, lying down on the bed.

Please, those moments that you want to kill—just save them for meditation. I don't want any other change in your life. I am not asking much: simply don't kill time. That time which you have been killing up to now, now let that time kill you!

THE POWER OF BEING NEUTRAL

You are not to do anything to become without thought, because *whatever* you will do will again be a thought. You have to learn to see the procession of thoughts, standing by the side of the road as if it does not matter to you what is passing by. Just the ordinary traffic—if you can take your thoughts in such a manner that they are not of much concern, then easily, slowly, the caravan of thoughts that has continued for thousands of years disappears.

You have to understand a simple thing, that giving attention is giving nourishment. If you don't give any attention, remain unconcerned, the thoughts start dying on their own. They don't have any other way to get energy, any other source of life. You are their energy, and because you go on seriously giving them attention, you think it is very difficult to be free from thought. It is the easiest thing in the world, but it has to be done in the right way.

The right way is just to stand by the side. The traffic goes on—let it go. Don't make any judgment of good and bad; don't appreciate, don't condemn. That is what is meant by being easy: it is all okay.

Our natural tendency is that if we have to become thoughtless, why not force the thoughts out? Why not throw them out? But by the very act of forcing them, you are giving them energy, you are giving them nourishment. You are taking note of them and you are making them important—so important that without throwing them out, you cannot meditate.

Just try to throw out any single thought, and you will see how difficult it is. The more you throw it the more it bounces back! It will enjoy the game very much, and you are finally going to be defeated. You have taken a wrong route.

You cannot repress any thought. The very process of repressing gives it energy, life, strength. And it weakens you because you become a defeated partner in the game. The easiest thing is not to force but just to be a witness. If a monkey comes, let him come. Just say "Hello!" and he will go. But don't tell him to go. Just be a witness that a monkey has come, or a thousand monkeys have come. What does it matter? It is none of your business. They may be going to some gathering, some religious festival, so let them go. It is none of your concern. And soon the crowd will disappear, seeing that "the person is not interested."

All your thoughts are in the same category. Never force any thought to go away; otherwise it will rebound with greater energy. And the energy is yours! You are on a self-defeating track. The more you push it away, the more it will come back.

THE ONLY WAY
to Be Without Thought

The only way—I say *the only way*—to be thoughtless is this: don't pay any attention. Just remain silently watching all kinds of things . . . monkeys and elephants, let them pass. Soon you will find an empty road, and when you find an empty road, you have found an empty mind—naturally. Everything outward and inward subsides and there is the tremendous silence that easiness brings.

I say out of my own experience that you can simply sit or lie down and let the thoughts pass by. They will not leave even a trace. Just don't get interested—and don't be *dis*interested,

either; just be neutral. To be neutral is to be easy, and to be neutral is to take back the very life force that you have given to your thoughts.

A man of no thought suddenly becomes so full of energy—energy that he had spread into thoughts unnecessarily. He was weak because he was nourishing thoughts, which leads nowhere. They promise—thoughts are politicians. They promise great things to come, but the moment they have power, they forget all their promises. This has been going on for centuries.

ACTIVATE YOUR AWARENESS

Awareness is simple, very innocent. Everyone has it, so it is not a question of achievement. One wrong question leads to another wrong question: first you ask what right awareness is, then you ask how to achieve it. You already have it.

When you see the sunset, are you not aware? When you see a rose flower, are you not aware? You are aware of the beautiful sunset, you are aware of the beautiful rose; all that is needed is that you become aware of your awareness, too. That is the only thing that has to be added, the only refinement.

You are aware of objects. You have to be aware of your subjectivity. When you are looking at a sunset, you are so absorbed in the beauty of the sunset that you completely forget that there is a greater beauty that is making it possible for you to know the beauty of the sunset—it is your awareness. But your awareness is focused on an object—the sunset, the sunrise, the moon. Drop the object and just remain engulfed in pure awareness, in silence, in peace. *Just be alert.*

THE METHOD
Just Watch

Awareness is a process of being more and more awake.

Whatever you are doing, you can do it like a robot, mechanically. Just watch: the way you are walking, is it alert or just a mechanical habit?

You have the awareness; it is just that you have not applied it. Apply it, so it becomes more and more sharp. Without application it has gathered dust.

In any act—walking, eating, drinking—whatever you are doing, make it a point that a current of awareness will always be running side by side. And your whole life will start having a mystical fragrance. And all awareness is right, and all unawareness is wrong.

A CUP OF MEDITATION

Whenever you find time, just for a few minutes relax the
breathing system, nothing else—there is no need to relax the
whole body. Sitting in the train or plane, or in the car, nobody
will become aware that you are doing something. Just relax the
breathing system. Let it be as when it is functioning naturally.
Then close your eyes and watch the breathing going in, coming
out, going in. . . .

Don't concentrate. If you concentrate you create trouble,
because then everything becomes a disturbance. If you try
to concentrate sitting in the car, then the noise of the car
becomes a disturbance, the person sitting beside you becomes a
disturbance.

Meditation is not concentration. It is simple awareness. You simply relax and watch the breathing. In that watching, nothing is excluded. The car is humming—perfectly okay, accept it. The traffic is passing—that's okay, part of life. The fellow passenger snoring by your side, accept it. Nothing is rejected. You are not to narrow down your consciousness.

Concentration is a narrowing down of your consciousness so you become one-pointed, but everything else becomes a competition. You are fighting everything else because you are afraid that the point may be lost. You may be distracted, and that becomes disturbing. Then you need seclusion, the Himalayas. You need a room where you can sit silently, nobody disturbing you at all.

No, that is not right—that cannot become a life process. It is isolating yourself. It does have some good results—you will feel more tranquil, calmer—but those results are temporary. When you don't have the conditions in which it can happen, it is lost.

A meditation in which you need certain prerequisites, in which certain conditions need to be fulfilled, is not meditation at all—because you will not be able to do it when you are dying. Death will be such a distraction. If life distracts you, just think about death. You will not be able to die meditatively, and then the whole thing is futile, lost. You will die again tense, anxious, in misery, in suffering, and you immediately create your next birth of the same type.

Let death be the criterion: anything that can be done even while you are dying is real—and that can be done anywhere, with no conditions necessary. If sometimes the conditions are good, enjoy them. If not, it makes no difference. Do it even in the marketplace.

And don't attempt to control the breath, because all control is from the mind, so meditation can never be a controlled thing. The mind cannot meditate. Meditation is something beyond the mind, or below the mind, but never within the mind. So if the mind remains watching and controlling, it is not meditation; it is concentration. Concentration is a mind effort. It brings the qualities of the mind to their peak. A scientist concentrates, a soldier concentrates; a hunter, a research worker, a mathematician, all concentrate. These are mind activities.

There is no need to make a fixed time for meditation. Use whatever time is available. When you have ten minutes in the bathroom, just stand under the shower and meditate. Meditate for short intervals—just five minutes—in the morning, in the afternoon, just four or five times a day, and you will see that it becomes constant nourishment. There is no need to do it for twenty-four hours.

Just a cup of meditation will do. No need to drink the whole river; just a cup of tea will do. And make it as easy as possible. Easy is right. Make it as natural as possible. And don't be always after it—just do it whenever you find time. Don't make a habit of it, because all habits are of the mind, and a real person in fact has no habits.

TAKE MEDITATION WITH YOU

"Is twenty minutes of meditation a day enough?"

You are such a miser—I never thought you were so miserly that you would give just twenty minutes in twenty-four hours. Not even twenty-four minutes!

And you have missed my basic standpoint completely. I don't want you to think of meditation within limits. *I want meditation to become your very life.* In the past this has been one of the fallacies: you meditate for twenty minutes, or you meditate three times a day, you meditate five times a day—different religions, but the basic idea is that a few minutes every day should be given to meditation.

And what will you do in the remaining time? Whatever you will gain in twenty minutes . . . What are you going to do in the remaining twenty-three hours and forty minutes? Something anti-meditative? Naturally, your twenty minutes will be defeated.

The enemies are so big, and you are giving so much juice and energy to the enemies but just twenty minutes for meditation.

No, meditation in the past has not been able to bring a rebellion in the world because of these fallacies. These fallacies are the reason I want you to look at meditation from a totally different standpoint. You can learn meditation for twenty minutes or forty minutes—learning is one thing—but then you have to carry whatever you have learned day in, day out. Meditation has to become just like your heartbeat. You cannot say, "Is it enough to breathe for twenty minutes every day?" The next day will never come! Even while you are asleep, you continue breathing. Nature has not left the essential functions of your body and life in your hands. Nature has not trusted you, because if breathing were in your hands, you would start thinking how much to breathe and whether it is right to breathe while you are sleeping. It looks a little odd doing two things together—sleeping and breathing. Breathing seems to be a kind of disturbance in sleeping. But then the sleep will be eternal!

Your heartbeat, your blood circulation, are not under your control. Nature has kept everything that is essential in its own hands. You are not reliable, you can forget, and then there is no time even to say, "I am sorry, I forgot to breathe. Just give me one more chance!" Even that much opportunity is not there.

But meditation is not part of your biology, your physiology, your chemistry; it is not part of the ordinary natural flow. If you want to remain just a human being for eternity, you can remain there. Nature has come to the point of evolution where more

than this is not needed by nature: you are perfectly capable of reproducing children, and that's enough. You will die, your children will continue. Your children will carry on the same stupidities that you were doing. Some will be joining the congregation, going to the churches; some other idiot will be giving sermons, and the whole thing will continue— don't be worried.

Nature has come to a point where now, unless you take individual responsibility, you cannot grow. More than this, nature cannot do. It has done enough: it has given you life, it has given you opportunity. Now it has left the question of how to use it up to you.

THE METHOD
Carry the Flavor of It

● ●

Meditation is your freedom, not a biological necessity. You can learn meditation in a certain period of time every day to strengthen it, to make it stronger—but carry the flavor of it the whole day.

First, when you awake, from the moment you wake up, immediately catch hold of the thread of remaining alert and conscious, because that is the most precious moment to catch the thread of consciousness. During the day you will forget many times—but the moment you remember, immediately start being alert. Never repent, because that is a sheer waste of time. Never repent, "My God, I forgot again!"

In my teachings there is no place for any repentance. Whatever has happened is gone. Now there is no need to waste time on it. Catch hold again of the thread of awareness. Slowly, slowly you will be able to be alert the whole day: an undercurrent of awareness in every act, in every movement, in everything that you are doing or not doing. Something underneath will be continuously flowing.

Even when you go to sleep, leave the thread only at the last moment when you cannot do anything because you are falling asleep. And this is one of the laws, that whatever is the last thing before you fall asleep will be the first thing when you wake up. Try it. Any small experiment will be enough to prove it.

Just repeat your own name while you are falling asleep: half awake, half asleep, go on repeating your name. Slowly, slowly you will forget to repeat it because the sleep will grow more and more and the thread will be lost. It is lost only because you are asleep, but underneath your sleep it continues. That's why in the morning when you wake up, just look around. The first thing you will remember will be your name. You will be surprised: "Why? What happened?" You slept eight hours, but there has been an undercurrent.

And as things become deeper and clearer, even in sleep you can remember that you are asleep. Sleep becomes almost just a physiological thing, and your spirit, your being, becomes a flame of awareness separate from it. It does not disturb your sleep; it simply makes your sleep very light. It is no longer the sleep of the old days, when your house was on fire and you went on sleeping. That was almost like a coma, you were so unconscious. Your sleep will become thin, a very light layer, and your inside will remain alert. Just as it has been alert in the day, it will finally be even more alert in the night because you are so silent, so relaxed, with the whole nuisance world completely silent.

You can continue for twenty minutes every day to learn meditation, to refresh, to give more energy and more roots—but don't be satisfied that that's enough. That's how the whole of humanity has failed, although the whole of humanity has tried in some way or other. But so few people have been successful that by and by, many people stopped even trying because success seemed to be so far away. But the reason is that just twenty minutes or ten minutes won't do.

I can understand that you have many things to do, so find time. But that time is not meditation, that time is only to refresh yourself—and then again you will have to work, earn, do your job, and a thousand and one things. Just remain alert of whether your awareness, your consciousness, is still there inside, or it has disappeared.

This continuity then becomes a garland of twenty-four hours.

YOUR ESSENTIAL NATURE

"What is awareness? Why is it lost, and how can it be regained? Are there any steps?"

Awareness is never lost. It simply becomes entangled with the other, with objects.

So the first thing to be remembered: it is never lost, it is your nature, but you can focus it on anything you want. When you get tired of focusing it on money, on power, on prestige, and that great moment comes in your life when you want to close your eyes and focus your awareness on its own source, on where it is coming from, on the roots—in a split second your life is transformed.

And don't ask what the steps are; there is only one step. The process is very simple. The step is only one: that is turning in.

In Judaism there is a rebellious school of mystery called Hasidism. Its founder, Baal Shem, was a rare being. In the middle of the night he was coming from the river—that was his routine, because at the river in the night it was absolutely calm and quiet. And he used to simply sit there, doing nothing—just watching his own self, watching the watcher.

This night, when he was coming back, he passed a rich man's house and the watchman was standing by the door. The watchman was puzzled because every night, at exactly this time, this man would come back from the river. He came out and he said, "Forgive me for interrupting but I cannot contain my curiosity

anymore. You are haunting me day and night, every day. What is your business? Why do you go to the river? I have followed you many times, and there is nothing—you simply sit there for hours, and in the middle of the night you come back."

Baal Shem said, "I know that you have followed me many times, because the night is so silent I can hear your footsteps. And every day I know you are hiding behind the gate. But it is not only that you are curious about me, I am also curious about you. What is your business?"

He said, "My business? I am a simple watchman."

Baal Shem said, "My God, you have given me the key word. This is my business, too!"

The watchman said, "But I don't understand. If you are a watchman you should be watching some house, some palace. What are you watching there, sitting in the sand?"

Baal Shem said, "There is a little difference: you are watching for somebody outside who may enter the palace; I simply watch this watcher. Who is this watcher? This is my whole life's effort; I watch myself."

The watchman said, "But this is a strange business. Who is going to pay you?"

He said, "It is such bliss, such a joy, such immense benediction, it pays itself profoundly. Just a single moment, and all the treasures are nothing in comparison to it."

The watchman said, "This is strange; I have been watching my whole life. I never came across such a beautiful experience. Tomorrow night I am coming with you. Just teach me. I know how to watch—it seems only a different direction is needed; you are watching in some different direction."

There is only one step, and that step is of direction, of dimension. Either we can be focused outside or we can close our eyes to the outside and let our whole consciousness be centered within. And you will know, because you *are* a knower, you *are* awareness. You have never lost it; you simply have your awareness entangled in a thousand and one things. Withdraw your awareness from everywhere and just let it rest within yourself, and you have arrived home.

IT IS IN YOUR HANDS

Many of our problems are just there because we have never looked at them, never focused our eyes on them to figure out what they are.

We have never looked at them face-to-face, never encountered them; and not looking at them is giving them energy. Being afraid of them is giving them energy, always trying to avoid them is giving them energy—because you are accepting them. Your very acceptance is their existence. Other than your acceptance, they don't exist.

So if you open your closets, take your light, and look at the skeletons, you will find they are dead. Nobody opens the cupboards in their unconscious, where they have many skeletons of many kinds. You yourself have put them there, and now you are afraid of them! But the reality is that they are dead; just open the doors, bring light, clean your closets, clean your mind of all the dead luggage that you are filled with—it is making your life really miserable, a hell. And nobody except you is responsible.

In the first place, you hide things that you should not. It is good to give them expression and release them. So first you hide them and just remain a hypocrite—that you are never angry, that you are never hateful, that you are never this, never that; but all that goes on collecting inside. Those are all dead things. They don't have any energy of their own, unless you give them energy. You have the source of energy. Whatever happens in your life needs your energy. If you cut off the source of energy . . . In other words, that's what I call identification; if you don't identify with anything, it immediately dies; it has no energy of its own.

And non-identification is the other side of watchfulness. Love the beauty of watchfulness and its immense capacity to transform you. Simply watch whatever it is, and you will suddenly see that there is nothing but a dead skeleton; it cannot do anything to you. But you can give energy to it, you can project energy onto it. Then a skeleton that cannot do anything can even kill you, can give you a heart attack. Just start trying to escape from it and you have given it reality; you have given it life.

Give life to things that are beautiful. Don't give life to ugly things. You don't have much time, much energy to waste. With such a small life, with such a small energy source, it is simply stupid to waste it in sadness, in anger, in hatred, in jealousy. Use it in love, use it in some creative act, use it in friendship, use it in meditation; do something with it that takes you higher. And the higher you go, the more energy sources become available to you.

At the highest point of consciousness, you are almost a god. But we don't allow that moment to happen to us. We go on falling downward into the darker and darker and darker spaces where we ourselves become almost living dead.

It is in your hands.

THE SEARCH FOR TRUTH

"When I listen to your stories of your early life, I never get the impression that you saw yourself as a spiritual seeker. Were you looking for enlightenment, or was enlightenment a by-product of an impeccable resolve to never compromise what you felt to be true?"

There are things that cannot be sought directly. The more valuable a thing is, the more indirectly you have to go into it. In fact, you have to do something else that simply prepares the situation around you—in which things like enlightenment, truth, can happen.

You cannot go seeking and searching for truth. Where will you go? Kabul? Kullu-Manali? Kathmandu? Goa? And then back home. All seekers of truth go this route, and come back home looking more foolish than before. They have not found anything.

Where will you go to seek truth? You don't know the way; there is no map, there is no direction available. Nobody knows what, where, when it is possible to realize truth.

The real seeker of truth never seeks truth. On the contrary, he tries to clean himself of all that is untrue, unauthentic, insincere—and when his heart is ready, purified, the guest comes. You cannot find the guest, you cannot go after him. He comes to you; you just have to be prepared. You have to be in a right attitude.

I have never been spiritual in the sense that you understand the word. I have never gone to the temples or the churches, or read scriptures, or followed certain practices to find truth, or worshipped God or prayed to God. That has not been my way at all. So certainly you can say that I was not doing anything spiritual. But to me, spirituality has a totally different connotation. It needs an honest individuality. It does not allow any kind of dependence. It creates a freedom for itself, whatever the cost. It is never in the crowd but alone, because the crowd has never found any truth. Truth has been found only in people's aloneness.

So my spirituality has a different meaning from your idea of spirituality. My childhood stories—if you can understand them—will point to all these qualities in some way or other. Nobody can call them spiritual. I call them spiritual because to me, they have given all that man can aspire to. While listening to my childhood stories you should try to look for some quality in it—not just the story but some intrinsic quality that runs like a thin thread through all of my memoirs. And that thin thread is spiritual.

Spiritual, to me, simply means finding oneself. I never allowed anybody to do this work on my behalf—because nobody can do this work on your behalf: you have to do it yourself. And you cannot do it directly, either; you have to create a certain milieu in which it happens. It is a happening; enlightenment, liberation, awakening, realization—all these words point toward absolutely one thing, and that is a happening.

That creates a kind of fear in many people: "If it is a happening, then what are we supposed to do? Whenever it will happen, it will happen." That is not so. It is a happening, but you can do much to prepare the ground for it to happen.

SILENCE WITHOUT EFFORT

Osho's talks—given extemporaneously and without notes except for a few jokes or excerpts from a text he is speaking about—are a meditation in themselves. Here's what he has to say about it:

The people who have known truth have chosen to speak rather than to write. All over the world—it cannot be just coincidence—in all the centuries, all over the world, they have chosen to speak. There is some fundamental significance in it. They all know the word cannot convey the truth, but the spoken word at least can have something alive in it.

My speaking is for the first time being used as a strategy to create silence in you.

I don't speak to teach something; I speak to create something. These are not lectures; these are simply a device for you to become silent, because if you are told to become silent without making any effort you will find great difficulty.

I don't have any doctrine; my talking is really a process of dehypnosis. Just listening to me, slowly, slowly you will be free of all the programs that the society has forced you to believe in.

I am not interested in any philosophy or any political ideology. I am interested directly in transforming you.

How to give people a taste of meditation was my basic reason to speak, so I can go on speaking eternally—it does not matter what I am saying. All that matters is that I give you a few chances to be silent, which you find difficult on your own in the beginning.

Something to try:

With Osho's recorded talks you can experience the art of listening with ease and wherever you are.

Many people find listening to these talks to be an essential key to bringing a relaxed, lucid, and sharp awareness into everyday life. OSHO Audiobooks are available where audiobooks are sold.

EPILOGUE

One truth I witness every day is that one cannot live without spirituality. Without spirituality something in a person remains empty and unfulfilled. This emptiness will start to ache, but you will find no way to fill it.

This is the state of modern man. I am not worried about it because in this state may lie the only hope for mankind's future and safety. Out of this very pain a thirst will be born, which, if given the right direction, can become a worldwide spiritual regeneration. For just as a dark night is followed by the rising sun, so the soul of man is very close to a new dawn.
"Osho, What are you doing here exactly?"

Selling water by the river.
Master Sogaku Harada died at the age of ninety-one. At his funeral service hung a piece of calligraphy written by him:

> For forty years I have been selling water
> by the bank of a river.
> Ho, ho!
> My labors have been wholly without merit.

That can only be said by a Zen master. First, he is selling water by the river where there is really no need. The river is flowing. You can simply jump into the river and drink your fill. But people are so foolish, they need somebody to sell water—even by the river.

Second, he says, "Ho, ho! My labors have been wholly without merit." That is a great statement. Zen masters say that if you do good, it is useless because basically everything is good. How can you do any more good? If you make people enlightened, what is the point of it? They were already enlightened; you are not doing anything new. "Ho, ho! My labors have been wholly without merit."

First we go on selling water by the side of the river. If you are a little intelligent you can jump in yourself. Finally, we know all effort is meaningless, in vain, because even if you become enlightened nothing is gained. You were always enlightened. But this can only be said by a Zen master. The insight is so deep; both things are profound. Nobody needs to be enlightened because everybody is already enlightened. It is such a ridiculous thing for people to keep trying to enlighten you.

It is so ridiculous for me to go on enlightening you every day. And you are stubborn: you will not become enlightened. I go on selling water by the river, and you pay for the water. You don't look at the river, and the river is flowing by the side. It has always been there. Before the thirst is created, the river was there. Before the desire, the fulfillment.

So you ask, "What are you doing here exactly?"

Selling water by the river. Ho, ho!

ABOUT OSHO

Osho's unique contribution to the understanding of who we are defies categorization. Mystic and scientist, a rebellious spirit whose sole interest is to alert humanity to the urgent need to discover a new way of living. To continue as before is to invite threats to our very survival on this unique and beautiful planet.

His essential point is that only by changing ourselves, one individual at a time, can the outcome of all our "selves"—our societies, our cultures, our beliefs, our world—also change. The doorway to that change is meditation.

Osho the scientist has experimented in and scrutinized all the approaches of the past and examined their effects on the modern human being and responded to their shortcomings by creating a new starting point for the hyperactive twenty-first-century mind: OSHO Active Meditations®.

Once the agitation of a modern lifetime has started to settle, "activity" can melt into "passivity," a key starting point of real meditation. To support this next step, Osho has transformed the ancient "art of listening" into a subtle contemporary methodology: the OSHO Talks. Here words become music, the listener discovers who is listening, and the awareness moves from what is being heard to the individual doing the listening. Magically, as silence arises, what needs to be heard is understood directly, free from the distraction of a mind that can only interrupt and interfere with this delicate process.

These thousands of talks cover everything from the individual quest for meaning to the most urgent social and political issues facing society today. Osho's books are not written but are transcribed from audio and video recordings of these extemporaneous talks to international audiences. As he puts it, "So remember: whatever I am saying is not just for you . . . I am talking also for the future generations."

Osho has been described by the *Sunday Times* in London as one of the "1000 Makers of the 20th Century" and by American author Tom Robbins as "the most dangerous man since Jesus Christ." *Sunday Mid-Day* (India) has selected Osho as one of ten people—along with Gandhi, Nehru, and Buddha—who have changed the destiny of India.

About his own work Osho has said that he is helping to create the conditions for the birth of a new kind of human being. He often characterizes this new human being as "Zorba the Buddha"—capable both of enjoying the earthy pleasures of a Zorba the Greek and the silent serenity of a Gautama the Buddha.

Running like a thread through all aspects of Osho's talks and meditations is a vision that encompasses both the timeless wisdom of all ages past and the highest potential of today's (and tomorrow's) science and technology.

Osho is known for his revolutionary contribution to the science of inner transformation, with an approach to meditation that acknowledges the accelerated pace of contemporary life.

His unique OSHO Active Meditations® are designed to first release the stresses of body and mind, inviting an experience of stillness and relaxation into daily life.

Two autobiographical works by the author are available:
Autobiography of a Spiritually Incorrect Mystic, St. Martin's Press, New York (book and eBook)
Glimpses of a Golden Childhood, OSHO Media International, Pune, India (book and eBook)

Follow Up:

WEB .... OSHO.com
OSHO ACTIVE MEDITATIONS® .... OSHO.com/meditate
YOUTUBE .... YouTube.com/OshoInternational
INSTAGRAM .... Instagram.com/oshointernational
MAGAZINE .... OSHOtimes.com
FACEBOOK .... Facebook.com/Osho.International
TWITTER .... Twitter.com/osho
MEDITATION RESORT .... osho.com/visit

Located in Pune, India, one hundred miles southeast of Mumbai, the OSHO International Meditation Resort is a holiday destination with a difference; spread over twenty-eight acres of spectacular Zen-gardens, offering around-the-clock and around-the-year meditation programs for every type of person, including the OSHO Active Meditations®, as well as personal transformation programs, all based in awareness, relaxation, celebration, and creativity. People from more than one hundred countries visit the meditation resort every year.

Also by the international bestselling author,

OSHO

Available everywhere books are sold

HARMONY BOOKS